Countries Around the World

Iran

Richard Spilsbury

Heinemann
LIBRARY
Chicago, Illinois

www.heinemannraintree.com
Visit our website to find out
more information about
Heinemann-Raintree books.

To order:
☎ Phone 888-454-2279
💻 Visit www.heinemannraintree.com
to browse our catalog and order online.

© 2012 Heinemann Library
an imprint of Capstone Global Library, LLC
Chicago, Illinois

Edited by Louise Galpine
Designed by Richard Parker
Original illustrations © Capstone Global Library, Ltd.
Illustrated by ODI
Picture research by Mica Brancic
Originated by Capstone Global Library, Ltd.
Printed by China Translation and Printing Company

15 14 13 12 11
10 9 8 7 6 5 4 3 2 1

Library of Congress Cataloging-in-Publication Data
Spilsbury, Richard, 1963-
  Iran / Richard and Louise Spilsbury.
    p. cm.—(Countries around the world)
  Includes bibliographical references and index.
  ISBN 978-1-4329-5208-2 (hc)—ISBN 978-1-4329-5233-4
(pb) 1. Iran—Juvenile literature. I. Spilsbury, Louise. II. Title.
  DS254.75.S65 2012
  955—dc22   2010038524

Acknowledgments

The author and publisher are grateful to the following for
permission to reproduce copyright material: Alamy pp. 10
(© Robert Harding Picture Library Ltd/Sybil Sassoon), 21 (©
Robert Harding Picture Library Ltd), 24, 25 (© dbimages), 30
(© Aurora Photos/Manca Juvan); Corbis pp. 5 (In Pictures/©
Manca Juvan), 9 (Sygma/© Alain Keler), 13 (© Michael S.
Yamashita), 15 (© Rob Howard), 17 (© Kazuyoshi Nomachi),
18 (© Theo Allofs), 19 (© Kaveh Kazemi), 20 (Reuters/© Caren
Firouz), 22 (Document Iran/© Mehdi Ghasemi), 23 (Reuters/
Yalda Moaiery/© Jamejamonline), 26 (Document Iran/©
Nikoo Harf Maher), 28 (Reuters/© Morteza Nikoubazl), 33
(Reuters/Morteza Nikoubazl), 35 (Reuters/© Anton Denisov/
X0168); 8 (Time Life Pictures/Dmitri Kessel), 27 (AFP Photo/
ISNA/Mona Hoobehfekr), 31 (Allsport/Stanley Chou), 32
(AFP Photo/Farzaneh Khademian); Shutterstock pp. 6 (©
Steba), 39 (© Valery Shanin), 46 (© granata1111).

Cover photograph of Khaju Bridge on the Zayandeh river,
early morning in Ispahan, Isfahan Province, Iran, reproduced
with permission of Corbis (Hemis/© Jean Heintz).

We would like to thank Peter Sluglett for his invaluable help in
the preparation of this book.

Contents

Some words are printed in bold, **like this**. You can find out what they mean by looking in the glossary.

Introducing Iran

What do you know about Iran? You might know that it is a country in the **Middle East**, located between Pakistan and Iraq. Iran is a country of deserts, but it also boasts lush coasts and jagged mountains. It is home to people with richly varied cultures. Some Iranians live in villages that have not changed much for hundreds of years. Others live in modern cities such as the capital, Tehran.

Islamic country

More than 98 percent of Iranians are **Muslims**. They belong mostly to the Shi'i **sect** of Islam. Most Muslims around the world belong to Islam's other major group, the Sunni sect. Both sects use the *Qur'an* as their holy book, but they differ in their leaders and **doctrines**. Religion is an important factor in the way the Iranian government treats its people.

Iran past and present

Iran has a rich and fascinating history. Iran today is a small part of a vast empire that once stretched across the Middle East. Iran influenced countries all around it through trade and sharing ideas. Some Western countries today view Iran with suspicion, as a troublemaker that supports **terrorism** and keeps the Middle East unstable. Many countries also recognize Iran's importance as a leading power in the Middle East.

How to say...

One of the most common phrases heard in Muslim countries is "*as-salam alaykum*" (ah-suh-lahm uh-LAY-koom). It is a greeting that means "peace be upon you." In Iran, people often say just *salaam* to each other. It is like saying "Hi."

The extensive mountains dominating large parts of Iran are just one of the less well-known aspects of the country.

History: Changing Rulers

Iran is one of the oldest **civilizations** on Earth. The first tribes that settled in the region, in around 2000 BCE included the Persians. Persian armies took control of the area in 550 BCE. This was the start of the Persian Empire. During the next 70 years, the empire spread into Egypt, India, and Europe.

King Darius built the Persian capital at Persepolis, and from there he led a more advanced society than most others of the time. Darius set up trading routes across the empire, including a paved road called the Royal Road that went all the way to the Mediterranean Sea. People all across the empire spoke Persian and used Persian money. The empire even had the first postal service in the world!

The ruins of ancient Persepolis still show the granduer of the Persian capital city.

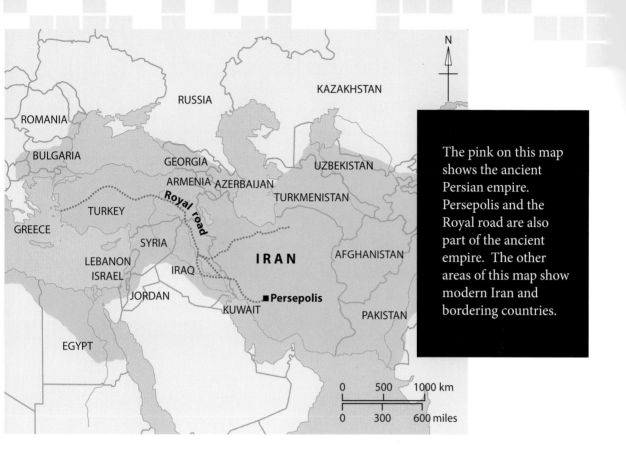

The pink on this map shows the ancient Persian empire. Persepolis and the Royal road are also part of the ancient empire. The other areas of this map show modern Iran and bordering countries.

Conquerors

After about 330 BCE, the empire was conquered by a series of rulers who wanted control of its land, resources, and trading routes. Arabs from the Arab Peninsula invaded in the 630s CE and introduced Islam as the region's major religion. A new **dynasty** of kings, or **shahs**, called the Safavids created the modern country of Iran in 1501. They established Shi'i Islam as the state religion, built palaces, **mosques**, schools, and public baths, and promoted arts such as carpet weaving.

SHAH ABBAS (1587–1629)

Shah Abbas was the greatest Safavid shah. He allowed different religions in the empire and was open to new ideas. For example, he established hospitals where people could have new medical treatments such as surgery under **anesthetic**. He also started state factories that produced silk carpets for **export**.

Times of change

By the late 19th century, Persia was making less from exports and needed money. So the shahs took payments from countries such as Russia and Britain in return for allowing them to search for oil. Beginning in the 1920s, Reza Shah modernized the country in some ways. The Persian government took control of the oil industry, built better roads, and gave women more rights. Reza Shah renamed the country "Iran" in 1935. Some Iranians soon felt that their country was becoming less religious and too influenced by Western ideas.

The Shah of Iran, seen with his son Prince Reza and wife Farah, at his lavish coronation in 1967. The way the royal family showed off their wealth and Western lifestyle was deeply unpopular among many Iranians.

How to say...

Allahu Akbar (a-LAH-hu AK-bah) means "God is great" in Arabic. Iranians say this phrase in many situations. They say it when they are praying, to show they are happy or approving, and even when stressed. It also appears as borders of the white section on the Iranian flag.

Revolution

In 1979, religious leaders including Ayatollah Ruhollah Khomeini led a bloody, Islamic **revolution**, forcing the shah from power. Thousands of people died during the revolution. The new government made big changes. It made health care available for all, but it also took away some rights from women and banned non-Islamic culture, such as Western music and art.

The revolution weakened Iran, and in 1980, Iraqi forces under President Saddam Hussein invaded. This started a war that lasted until 1988 and killed about one million people. Since then, Iran has grown into an important power in the Middle East.

Iranians carry a vast banner of their new leader Ayatollah Khomeini during the 1979 revolution.

Population

Today, Iran has a population of around 67 million, which is about twice the population of Canada. The average Iranian is just over 26 years old. Traditionally, most young adults stayed in the village of their birth to work. Today, more than two-thirds of Iranians live in large towns and cities, where there is a greater variety of jobs and they can earn more money.

These Quashqai nomads travel on mules between grazing lands in Iran as their tribe has done for thousands of years.

Daily life

Some Iranians are **nomads**. This means they travel around the country moving herds of livestock to different grazing lands. For example, the Qashqai people move to pastures near the Persian Gulf when central Iran grows too cold. They move back in summer when the Gulf lands are too warm. Some Iranian nomads live in black tents that they carry around on camels or motorbikes!

Varied people and language

The Iranian population is made up of many **ethnic groups**. More than half of Iranians are Persians who speak the Persian language. In Persian, the name of the language is Farsi. Modern Persian is similar to the Persian spoken at the time of King Darius, with the addition of newer words from other languages, such as "television."

Iranian Turks, or Azeri, live in northwestern Iran and are the descendants of Turks who invaded in the 11th century. Kurdish people live in Iran, Turkey, Iraq, Syria, and other countries. Iranian Kurds are somewhat independent of government rule. This is partly because they follow Sunni beliefs and were once **persecuted** by Shi'i Muslims.

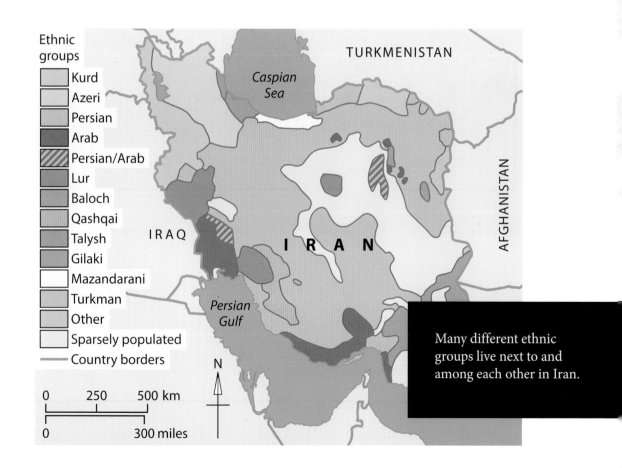

Ethnic groups

- Kurd
- Azeri
- Persian
- Arab
- Persian/Arab
- Lur
- Baloch
- Qashqai
- Talysh
- Gilaki
- Mazandarani
- Turkman
- Other
- Sparsely populated
- —— Country borders

0   250   500 km

0   300 miles

Many different ethnic groups live next to and among each other in Iran.

Regions and Resources: Deserts, Heat, and Oil

Iran is about twice the size of the state of Texas. It is made up of a high, flat desert **plateau** surrounded by a ring of mountains. The Zagros is Iran's main mountain range. Some Iranian deserts are sandy or gravelly. Others are crusted with salt from dried-up salt marshes. The northern Iranian coast borders the Caspian Sea, the largest lake in the world. Iran's warm southern coast is on the Persian Gulf and the Gulf of Oman. Most Iranian rivers are small, and many of the lakes are salty.

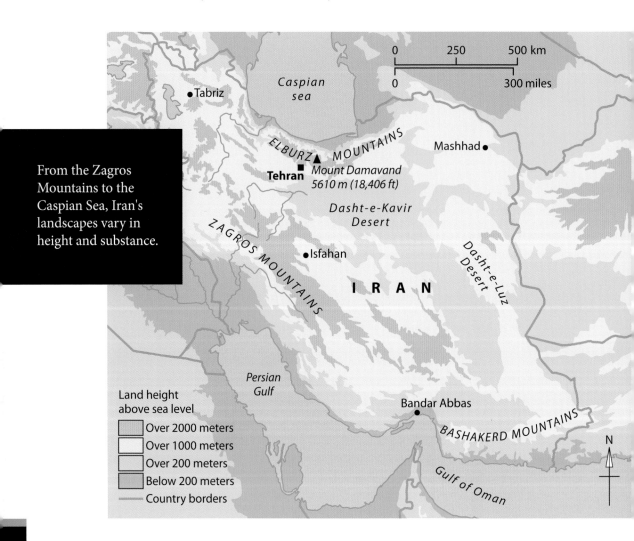

From the Zagros Mountains to the Caspian Sea, Iran's landscapes vary in height and substance.

Caspian sea

Tabriz

ELBURZ MOUNTAINS

Mashhad

Tehran ■ Mount Damavand 5610 m (18,406 ft)

Dasht-e-Kavir Desert

ZAGROS MOUNTAINS

Isfahan

Dasht-e-Luz Desert

I R A N

0   250   500 km
0   300 miles

Persian Gulf

Bandar Abbas

BASHAKERD MOUNTAINS

Gulf of Oman

N

Land height above sea level

- Over 2000 meters
- Over 1000 meters
- Over 200 meters
- Below 200 meters
- Country borders

Many of the traditional houses in the desert city of Yazd have tall wind towers, or badgirs, that use wind to cool air inside so it does not get too hot for people to live there.

Climate

Iran has a varied climate. Both baking hot deserts and snowy ski resorts lie just a few hours from Tehran. During the summer, temperatures can rise to 50°C (122°F) in the center of the country and in the southwest. Traditional houses sometimes have tall wind towers, or *badgirs*, that use wind to cool air inside. In the mountains, temperatures can drop to –40°C (–40°F) in winter. Iran is generally dry. An average of just 5 centimetres (2 inches) of rain falls each year in the desert near the Pakistan border. As much as 200 centimeters (80 inches) falls each year near the Caspian Sea.

Daily life

In Iran, a regular strong wind called the *seistan* blows during summer from the north-west. It is known as the "wind of 120 days" because it blows for four months. The *seistan* sometimes stirs up vast dust storms. These winds can blast sand so hard it strips paint from cars!

Provinces

Iran is divided into 31 regions called **provinces**. Each province has its own local government. The largest province in Iran is Sistan and Baluchistan in the southeast. This province is quite poor and home to many nomadic people. One of the smallest provinces, Qom, is near Tehran. It is named after its major city, which is important as a center for the study of Shi'i Islam.

Natural resources

The main natural resources in Iran are **fossil fuels**. A British company which discovered oil in Iran in 1908 and set up a company to drill and sell it, later became British Petroleum, or BP. Today Iran controls its own oil reserves, which are in the southwest and the Persian Gulf. It is the fourth-largest producer of oil in the world, and the fifth-largest producer of **natural gas**. Iran also mines metals such as copper, iron, zinc, and chromium.

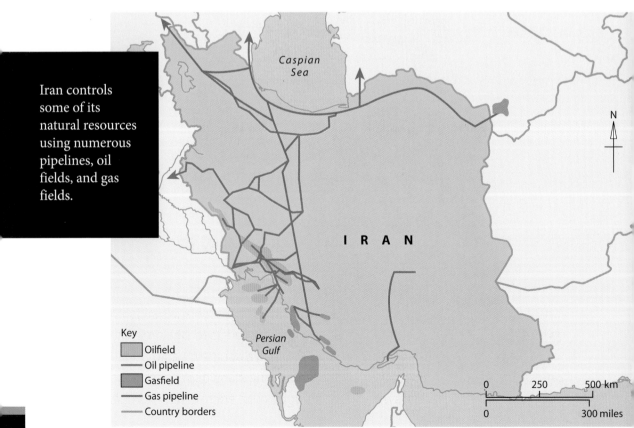

Iran controls some of its natural resources using numerous pipelines, oil fields, and gas fields.

Caspian Sea

N

IRAN

Persian Gulf

Key

Oilfield
Oil pipeline
Gasfield
Gas pipeline
Country borders

0   250   500 km

0   300 miles

Gilan province next to the Caspian Sea is warm and damp with many forested mountains. It is a center for rice, fruit, and nut farming.

Daily life

Iran is rich in oil, yet it has to **import** more than one third of the gas and diesel fuel needed to run the nation's cars from other countries. The reason is that it has few of the **refineries** needed to change its own oil into useful fuels. Gas stations regularly run out of fuel because the government does not buy enough to meet demand.

Economy

Before oil was discovered in Iran, its main exports were agricultural products. These included dried fruit and nuts and handmade carpets made with wool from nomads' sheep. Today, Iranian carpets are still prized for their quality and exported to many countries. But about 80 percent of the total value of Iranian exports now comes from oil and chemicals such as **fertilizers**, which are derived from oil. Iran's soil is poorer than it once was, so the country has to import food to feed its people.

Sanctions

Sanctions are punishments made to stop others doing things. Countries in the **United Nations**, including the United States and Germany, have enacted sanctions against Iran to stop it from developing **nuclear power**. They believe Iran will use the technology to build nuclear weapons. The sanctions include not letting Iran import airplane fuel and parts, and preventing Iranian banks from borrowing money from foreign banks. Because of this, ordinary Iranians cannot borrow money easily.

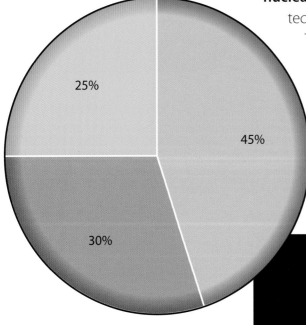

25%

45%

30%

Most Iranians are employed in the Services, which means they provide a service to someone. People who work in Industry make a product, and those in Agriculture grow products.

Key

Services

Industry

Agriculture

These Qashqai women work in groups to weave large carpets by hand. Even so it takes many months to finish each carpet.

Work

Most Iranians work in service industries. Service industry workers, such as government employees and shopkeepers, provide a service for others rather than making, growing, or mining a product. More than one-tenth of working-age Iranians are unemployed because there are not enough jobs for the growing population. Some move to other countries to find work.

Daily life

Some essential goods in Iran are kept cheap by government **subsidies** that pay part of the cost. For example, a loaf of bread costs about 1,000 *rials*, which is just over 10 cents!

Wildlife: Variety and Threats

A wide variety of wildlife lives in Iran's many **ecosystems**. Steppe wolves, wild goats, and boars roam the mountains and forests. Typical desert and semi-desert animals range from jackals to wild asses to lizards. Lakes are important feeding places for visiting birds such as cranes and geese. Trees called **mangroves** grow in the warm, shallow waters edging the Persian Gulf. The network of mangrove roots provides sheltered areas where young fish, shrimp, and turtles live.

Threatened species

Several Iranian species are threatened or **endangered** by too much hunting and fishing. Large fish called sturgeon living in the Caspian Sea are killed for their eggs, which people eat as **caviar**. Iran exports a lot of caviar but most comes from sturgeon grown on fish farms. Wild sturgeon are protected in Iran, but they sometimes swim into parts of the Caspian Sea controlled by other countries, such as Russia, where they are not as well protected.

The wild ass, or onager, is related to the donkey. It feeds on dry grasses and bushes in the barren lands of the Iranian plateau.

How to say...

Shir means "lion" in Persian. The lion represents bravery, strength, and greatness and was a symbol of the shahs. Lions appeared on the Persian flag from the 1400s until the Islamic revolution. Asiatic lions once ranged across Iran, but because of hunting, they disappeared from the country by the 1940s.

Protecting wildlife

People in Iran are working in a variety of ways to protect wildlife. The Iranian Cheetah Society is using talks to schoolchildren and information displays at zoos to teach young Iranians about big cats such as Persian leopards and desert cheetahs. It encourages Iranians to view big cats as tourist attractions and important parts of ecosystems, rather than as enemies that kill livestock and which therefore should be hunted.

The Iranian government protects wildlife in reserves and national parks. These protected regions total about one-twentieth of the country's area. For example, game wardens in the Naybandan Wildlife **Refuge** in Yazd province protect a large population of desert cheetahs from hunting. The refuge also protects rare Persian gazelles and wild sheep.

This desert cheetah was captured by a poacher as a cub, but rescued by the Iranian Department of the Environment and cared for in a Tehran zoo.

Sheep and goats are more common than cattle in Iran as they can survive even in poor pasturelands, as here near Shiraz. However, they can easily strip such areas of all vegetation.

People and the environment

Some human activities in Iran damage the land. Farmers sometimes keep too many livestock on dry grassland. The **livestock** eat all the plants and trample the soil so other plants will not grow there. The soil also dries out and blows away as dust, so the overgrazing is turning more farmland into desert. Sewage, oil, and chemicals used in industries such as mining, are also polluting the water supplies.

Most of Iran's freshwater is groundwater, which lies under the surface of the earth in spaces between the rocks. During the Persian Empire, people started to dig channels called *qanats* to take the groundwater into settlements. Today, there are 270,000 kilometers (170,000 miles) of *qanats*. But Iranians are using more water than in the past, so groundwater supplies are running out.

Infrastructure: Making Iran Work

Some countries have a king, but Iran has a supreme leader instead. The supreme leader is appointed by a group of religious leaders called the Assembly of Experts. He interprets the *Qur'an* to decide how the country should be run.

Elected leaders

Every four years, the people of Iran elect a president from a list of **candidates** approved by the supreme leader. The current supreme leader, Ayatollah Ali Khamenei, came to office in 1989. The president meets with international leaders and works to improve the nation's economy. He is in charge of a **parliament** of 290 politicians who represent different regions and ethnic groups.

Iranian president Mahmoud Ahmadinejad was elected in 2005 and again in 2009. Riots erupted after the 2009 election when Khamenei approved Ahmadinejad's victory, because many Iranians believe his opponent, Mir Mousavi, got more votes.

Mahmoud Ahmadinejad giving a speech in front of an image of the current supreme leader, Ayatollah Ali.

Female members of Iran's Basij militia, part of the Revolutionary Guards, training in how to control riots using sticks and tear gas.

Military forces

More than half a million Iranians are in the military. About a quarter of them belong to a group of security police called the Revolutionary Guards. The Revolutionary Guards protect the supreme leader and other officials and stop unrest in the country, such as during the 2009 elections. They also help the regular army when it is defending the country.

MAHMOUD AHMADINEJAD (1956–)

The president of Iran, Mahmoud Ahmadinejad took part in the Islamic revolution when he was a student. He joined the Revolutionary Guards and later became mayor of Tehran. Ahmadinejad is controversial because of his nuclear power program, his comments about other countries, especially Israel, and his possible support of international terrorism.

Health care

The Iranian government provides free health care at health centers in villages throughout the country. *Behvarzan*, or health volunteers, run the health centers. They treat minor problems and give advice on diet and cleanliness. The health centers have improved the lives of the people of Iran. Iranians live an average of 71 years, and only 36 Iranian babies die out of every 1,000 born. These figures are better than for most other nearby countries. People with problems that *behvarzan* cannot treat are sent to one of 700 hospitals or clinics. People usually have to pay to see a doctor there.

As in other countries, ambulances in Iran (like this one in Esfahan) help transport sick or injured people to the hospital.

YOUNG PEOPLE

Behvarzan often visit village schools. They check each child's health, and advise them how to stay healthy. Girls who are at least 16 years old and young men who have already served in the army can apply to become *behvarzan*. If selected, they receive free government training.

Iranian women can do many of the things men do, but are expected to dress and behave modestly in public.

Religious law

The law in Iran is based on the rules of ancient Islamic law, called Shar'ia law, and the recommendations of senior judges appointed by the supreme leader. Shari'a covers crimes, family disputes, and public behavior. Some Iranian laws are different for men and women. For example, women are expected to cover their bodies from public view by wearing *hijabs* (headscarves) or face-covering robes called *chadors*, and loose clothing. Some punishments for breaking laws in Iran are very harsh. For example, people may be beaten with sticks, have stones thrown at them until they are killed, or have their fingers cut off.

Education

Iran has more than 100,000 schools that employ nearly one million teachers. Education is free in schools run by the government, but some Iranian families pay for their children to attend private schools. Iranian girls and boys go to separate schools. Boys always have male teachers, and girls have female teachers. Some schools have school uniforms. For example, all girls at an elementary school may wear loose blue tops and trousers, or matching *hijabs*.

Children start school when they are five years old. School starts at around 7 a.m. and ends at lunchtime. Students learn reading, math, and science. When they are about 13, children go to secondary school. In secondary school, they study either job skills, such as farming or plumbing, or subjects that will help them get into college, such as science, law, and languages. Young people study the *Qur'an* and learn more about Islam at classes held in mosques or in special religious colleges called *madrassas*.

Iranian girls at their first day of school in Tehran, Iran.

Iranian high school students sitting for their university entrance examination in Tehran in 2009.

YOUNG PEOPLE

Iran has 80 state universities, and young Iranians need to take the *Konkur*, or university entrance exam, to get in. This difficult exam lasts 4.5 hours. Many parents pay for extra teaching to help their children. They do this because only one-tenth of those taking the *Konkur* are admitted to college.

Culture: Festivals, Food, and Fun

Most Iranian holidays are religious. On the birthday of Muhammad, the founder of Islam, people tell stories about his life. During the month of Ramadan, Iranians **fast** during the daytime to become better Muslims. Families often picnic together for *Nawruz*, a festival celebrating the new year.

A waiter prepares food to be served at a restaurant during celebrations for a festival in central Tehran.

Food

Most Iranians eat a healthy diet with lots of fresh vegetables and fruit. They eat lamb and beef, but they do not eat pork or ham, because Islam forbids eating pigs. Fruit such as dates are common for dessert, and Iranians occasionally eat ice cream and cakes. Favorite drinks include black tea and *dugh*, which is made from yogurt and salted water.

Kukuye Sabzi recipe

Iranians often eat this baked omelette at Nawruz. Have an adult help you with this recipe.

Ingredients

- 6 eggs
- 4 onions
- 2 leeks
- 4 ounces of spinach
- handful of parsley and thyme
- salt
- pepper
- oil or butter for greasing
- chopped nuts (optional)

Instructions

Finely chop the onions, leeks, spinach, parsley, and thyme. Beat the eggs in a large bowl, and add salt, pepper, and the vegetables and herbs. Grease an oven dish, and pour the mixture in. Top with chopped nuts if you like. Bake for 30–40 minutes in a 165 °C (325 °F) oven until lightly browned.

Daily Life

Here are some typical meals Iranians eat through the day.

Breakfast: flatbread, cheese, jam, egg

Lunch: meat stews containing vegetable or fruit; *kebabs*, served with rice

Evening meal: leftovers from lunch, flatbread, cheese, salad

Meeting and greeting

When Iranians of the same sex meet at a restaurant or gathering, they greet each other by shaking hands or kissing cheeks, and they often hold hands. But contact like this between a male and a female is acceptable only between young children or relatives.

When visiting an Iranian's home, it is polite to refuse tea when it is first offered. Visitors only accept the tea after the host insists. This Iranian system of politeness is known as *taarof*.

Sports

Iran's traditional national sport is *pahlavani* wrestling. Contestants build up strength using weighted clubs and exercises and then fight to see who is strongest in holding down an opponent. This sport began as military training in pre-Islamic times.

Skiing and snowboarding are popular at resorts such as Shamshak on snowy slopes of the mountains near Tehran. Resorts are more socially relaxed than other parts of Iran so young men and women can enjoy the slopes together.

Soccer is the most popular modern spectator sport in Iran, and the country has the fourth-largest soccer stadium in the world. Many young Iranians play *futsal*, a type of indoor soccer. Women usually play sports separately from men and are required to wear clothing that keeps them modestly covered.

Vahid Shamsaee of Iran at the Tiger 5s International Futsal Tournament held at the Singapore Indoor Stadium, Singapore.

VAHID SHAMSAEE

Vahid Shamsaee is the most famous *futsal* player in Iran and elsewhere in Asia. He has scored more goals in international matches than any other *futsal* player in the world. Like many Iranian *futsal* stars, he learned his skills playing in the streets and parks of Tehran.

Music and art

Traditional Iranian music uses instruments such as lutes, flutes, fiddles, tambourines, and drums. Iran's leaders have banned music such as rap and heavy metal because it focuses on Western lifestyles. But many young people still listen to it on the Internet or at illegal concerts, despite the threat of police raids. One of the most popular pop stars is Hichkas, a hip-hop artist who has never officially been allowed to release a CD.

Iranian guitarist and singer Sharareh Farnejad of Iranian rock band Arian performs in a Tehran concert hall in 2007.

Traditional Iranian arts include miniature painting, which shows the adventures of ancient Persian rulers and heroes. **Calligraphy**, another traditional art, is based on writing, especially religious writing. It is often found in books and on walls of mosques. Today, some Iranian artists still use miniature and calligraphy techniques for newer subjects. For example, Farah Ossouli paints imaginary lives of heroines.

The media

Iran has 20 daily newspapers and different news, sports, and talk show channels on TV. But the government controls all forms of media—newspapers, books, films, TV, and radio. Most foreign films are banned in Iran. Iranians find ways around the bans, however. Many people have satellite dishes, so millions of Iranians watch foreign TV channels like MTV and BBC Persian TV.

Iranians at the public screening of a movie in 2006 about the astronaut and businesswoman Anousheh Ansari.

YOUNG PEOPLE

By law, Iranian women are not allowed to sing in public, but many sing in private. Some take private singing classes and others, such as a young rapper named Salomi, make videos of their songs to show on the Internet.

Iran Today

Iranians today are proud of their ancient culture. Yet violence after the 2009 presidential elections proved that many Iranians, especially young people, want to modernize their country. They want a government that is less tightly controlled by strict religious leaders, as in the period before the 1979 revolution. This change would allow people more freedom to express their ideas and make choices, not just on the Internet, but also in public. Such a change would have a big impact, especially on Iranian women.

Changing relations

Many people around the world believe Iran has the right to develop nuclear power, despite the concerns of some Western countries. After all, no one denied those same Western countries the right to do exactly the same thing. But many Iranians are unhappy at how their country is being isolated. Sanctions keep many Iranians in poverty. Iran's dependence on oil means that the money they get from exports varies as the price of oil changes. If Iran had better relations with the Western nations, and especially the United States, it might be able to develop other industries such as tourism. This might improve life for many of its citizens.

ANOUSHEH ANSARI (1966–)

Anousheh Ansari moved from Iran to the United States as a teenager. She studied hard and became rich through developing phone and computer technology. In 2006, she became the first Iranian astronaut and the first Muslim in space. Her achievements have inspired many Iranian girls.

Anousheh Ansari, the world's first female space tourist, smiles during a news conference in the Star City space centre outside Moscow October 2, 2006.

Fact File

Official Name: Islamic **Republic** of Iran

Government: Islamic republic

Capital city: Tehran

Largest cities: Tehran, Mashhad, Isfahan, Shiraz, Tabriz

Official language: Persian

Bordering countries: Afghanistan, Armenia, Azerbaijan, Iraq, Pakistan, Turkey, Turkmenistan

Area: 1,648,195 square kilometers (636, 372 square miles)

The population of Iran has grown steadily over the years, especially since 1980.

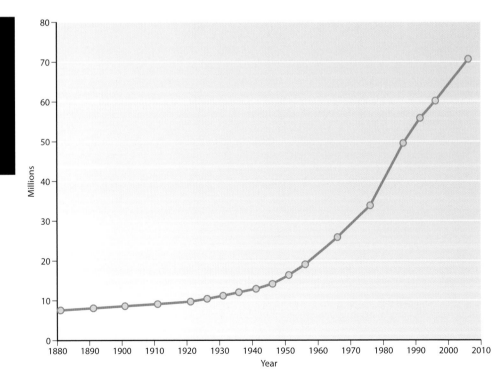

The average literacy rate in Iran is 77%. The literacy rate for males is slightly higher than that of females.

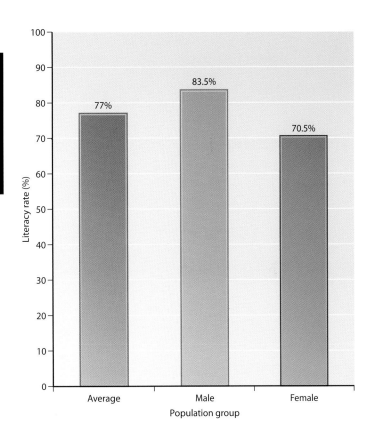

Highest point: Mount Damavand, 5,671 meters (18,606 feet)

Lowest point: Caspian Sea, 28 meters below sea level
(84 feet below sea level)

Population: 66,429,284 (July 2010 estimated)

Prominent Iranians: Sima Bina, folk musician (1944–)
Ibn Sina (Avicenna), ancient doctor (980-1037)
Rasoul Khadem, Olympic wrestler (1972–)
Samira Makhmalbaf, film director (1980–)
O-hum, rock group (1999–)
Pierre Omidyar, founder of Ebay (1967–)

Fact File

Main imports: Raw materials, food, consumer goods

Main exports: Oil, chemicals, fruits, nuts, carpets

Main trading partners: China, United Arab Emirates, Japan, India, Germany, South Korea

Poverty rate: 18 percent

Currency: *Rial*

National anthem

Iran's national anthem was adopted in 1990 and the music was written by Hassan Riahi.

Upwards on the horizon rises the Eastern Sun,
The sight of the true Religion.
Bahman—the brilliance of our Faith.
Your message, O Imam, of independence and freedom
is imprinted on our souls.
O Martyrs! The time of your cries of pain rings in
our ears.
Enduring, continuing, eternal,
The Islamic Republic of Iran.

Mosques often feature beautiful decorations.

Timeline

BCE means "before the common era." When this appears after a date it refers to the number of years before the Christian religion began. BCE dates are always counted backward.

CE means "common era." When this appears after a date, it refers to the time after the Christian religion began.

BCE

2000	People first settle in the Iran region.
522–486	King Darius rules the Persian Empire.

CE

636	Arabs invade, bringing Islam to the region.
800s	The Modern Persian language develops .
Early 1200s	Invasion by Mongol forces of Genghis Khan.
1501	Safavid rulers make Shi'i Islam the state religion.
1908	Oil is discovered in Iran.
1925	Parliament votes to make prime minister Reza Khan the ruler of the country.
1935	Reza Shah changes the name of the country from Persia to Iran.
1941	Britain and Russia occupy Iran. They force out Reza Shah and place his son, Mohammad Reza Pahlavi, in charge.
1951	Iran tries to nationalize its oil.
1963	The shah starts to modernize and Westernize the country.
1979	The shah is forced from power; the Islamic Republic of Iran is created.

1980	Iraq invades Iran, starting the Iran–Iraq War.
1989	Ayatollah Ali Khamenei is appointed the supreme leader.
1995	The United States imposes oil and trade sanctions on Iran.
2002	Construction begins on Iran's first nuclear reactor.
2005	Mahmoud Ahmadinejad is elected president.
2009	Ahmadinejad is reelected president, but rival candidates say vote count was not accurate. At least 30 people are killed in protests, and more than 1,000 are arrested.

Glossary

anesthetic drug that stops people or animals from feeling pain

BCE means "before the common era." When this appears after a date it refers to the number of years before the Christian religion began. BCE dates are always counted backward.

calligraphy art of beautiful handwriting

candidate person running for political office

caviar highly prized fish eggs

civilization way in which a society organizes itself

CE means "common era." When this appears after a date, it refers to the time after the Christian religion began.

doctrine principle in a system of belief

dynasty line of rulers from the same family

ecosystem community of living things and their environment, which work as a unit

endangered at some risk of dying out

ethnic group people with distinct, shared cultural traditions

export send goods to another country for sale

fast go without eating

fertilizer chemical substance put on soil to make plants grow better

fossil fuel type of fuel, such as coal or oil, that formed underground from plant or animal remains

import bring in from another country for selling

kebab cubes of meat cooked on skewers

livestock animals that are kept on a farm, such as sheep or cows

mangrove trees that grow in salty water

Middle East region covering southwest Asia and northeast Africa

mosque building where Muslims worship

Muslim person who follows the religion of Islam

natural gas gas that can be ignited and burned; usually found underground near petroleum

nomad someone who travels from place to place rather than settling down

nuclear power electricity that is created from atomic energy rather than burning fossil fuels

parliament group of people elected to make decisions and laws in a country

persecute treat someone cruelly

plateau raised flat area of land

province region of a country with its own local government

refinery building where a product such as oil is made pure

refuge place that provides shelter or protection

republic nation in which the supreme power rests with citizens who can vote

revolution when large numbers of people try to change the government, through either peaceful or violent protest

sanction limit on contact and trade with a country to force it to change its policies

sect religious group consisting of members with similar beliefs

shah king of Iran

subsidy aid given by the government to people or groups

terrorism violence used to force a government to change

United Nations association of most of the world's countries, which aims to improve economic, political, and social conditions worldwide

Find Out More

Books

Bahmani, Bruce. *Rostam: Tales from the Shahnameh* (Persian Book of Kings). Los Angeles: Hyperwerks, 2005.

Fast, April. *Iran the People*. New York: Crabtree, 2010.

Gray, Leon. *Iran*. Washington, DC: National Geographic, 2008.

Lee, Howard. *Jamshid and the Lost Mountain of Light*. Charleston, SC: Book Surge, 2008.

Satrapi, Marjane. *Persepolis*. New York: Vintage, 2008.

Websites

www.thebritishmuseum.ac.uk/forgottenempire/
Learn about ancient Persia.

http://web.archive.org/web/20071203180622rn_1/personal.ee.surrey.ac.uk/Personal/F.Mokhtarian/recipes/
To view a wide range of recipes from Iran.

http://tehran.stanford.edu/
See examples of calligraphy and carpet weaving, and hear samples of traditional music.

DVDs

Persopolis (2008), directed by Vincent Paronnaud and Marjane Satrapi. This award-wining movie is an animated version of the acclaimed graphic novel.

Mystic Iran (2004), directed by Aryana Farshad
A documentary looking at generally unseen aspects of Iran.

Places to visit

National Museum of Iran, Tehran

See a wide range of objects from before and after the Arab invasion.
http://www.nationalmuseumofiran.ir

British Museum, London, England

See ancient objects and copies of Persepolis sculptures.
http://www.britishmuseum.org

Victoria and Albert Museum, London, England

The museum exhibits good Persian carpets and other Persian art
http://www.vam.ac.uk

Louvre, Paris, France

The museum houses some Safavid miniature paintings.
http://www.louvre.fr

Metropolitan Museum of Art, New York, NY, United States

You can see Safavid miniatures and books.
http://www.metmuseum.org

Topic tools

You can use these topic tools for your school projects. Trace the flag and map on to a sheet of paper, using the thick black outlines to guide you, then color in your pictures. Make sure you use the right colors for the flag!

The red tulip on Iran's flag is made of letters that spell Allah, or "God," in Persian. The flower symbolizes the blood of people who died during the revolution.

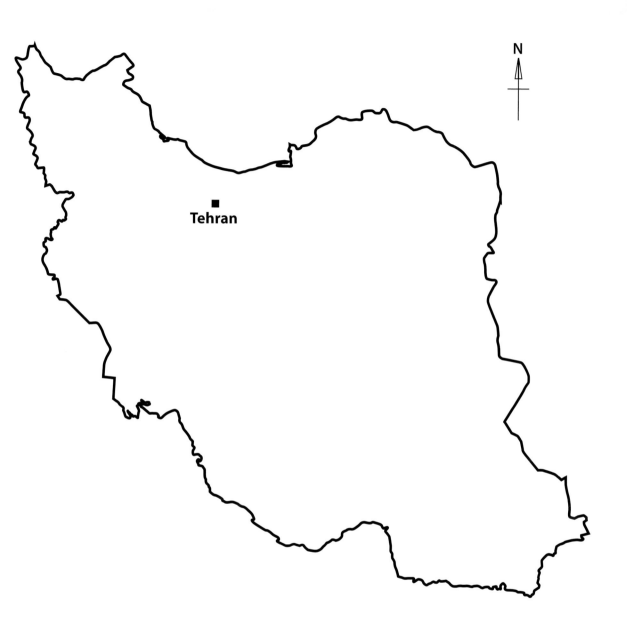

N

Tehran

Index

Titles in the series

Afghanistan	978 1 4329 5195 5
Brazil	978 1 4329 5196 2
Chile	978 1 4329 5197 9
Costa Rica	978 1 4329 5198 6
Cuba	978 1 4329 5199 3
Czech Republic	978 1 4329 5200 6
England	978 1 4329 5201 3
Estonia	978 1 4329 5202 0
France	978 1 4329 5203 7
Germany	978 1 4329 5204 4
Haiti	978 1 4329 5205 1
Hungary	978 1 4329 5206 8
India	978 1 4329 5207 5
Iran	978 1 4329 5208 2
Iraq	978 1 4329 5209 9
Italy	978 1 4329 5210 5
Latvia	978 1 4329 5211 2
Lithuania	978 1 4329 5212 9
Mexico	978 1 4329 5213 6
Pakistan	978 1 4329 5214 3
Poland	978 1 4329 5215 0
Scotland	978 1 4329 5216 7
Wales	978 1 4329 5217 4
Yemen	978 1 4329 5218 1